# JACKSON, VAN BUREN, HARRISON, TYLER, AND POLK

*by*

MICHAEL WEBER

VOLUME

## 3

ROURKE CORPORATION, INC.

VERO BEACH, FLORIDA 32964

Printed in the United States of America.

A Blackbirch Graphics book.
*Series Editor:* Tanya Lee Stone

**Photo Credits**
Cover: Andrew Jackson, William H. Harrison, and James K. Polk, National Portrait Gallery; Martin Van Buren, Library of Congress; John Tyler, National Portrait Gallery, Smithsonian Institution/Art Resource, NY.
Pages 4, 7, 18, 21, 24 (bottom), 34, 36, 42, 50, 52, 54, 55: North Wind Picture Archives; page 6: New York Public Library, Stokes Collection; pages 10, 11, 12, 22, 24 (top), 32, 44: National Portrait Gallery; pages 15, 16, 19, 26, 28, 29, 31, 35, 41, 47, 48: Library of Congress; page 38: National Portrait Gallery, Smithsonian Institution/Art Resource, NY.

**Library of Congress Cataloging-in-Publication Data**

Weber, Michael, 1945-
    The complete history of our presidents / Michael Weber, Richard Steins, Eileen Lucas.
        p. cm.
    Includes bibliographical references and index.
    Summary: Discusses the political lives and times of the men who served as United States presidents, their administrations, and the events which occurred during their tenures.
    ISBN 0-86593-405-3 (set)
    1. Presidents—United States—Juvenile literature.
[1. Presidents.]   I. Steins, Richard.   II. Lucas, Eileen.
III. Title.
E176.1.W365      1997
973'.099—DC20                                    96-14831
                                                  CIP
                                                   AC
                                                  Rev.

# TABLE OF CONTENTS

*Railroads played a big part in the transportation revolution in America during the first half of the 1800s.*

*1*

★  ★  ★

# A Time of Change

Five presidents—Andrew Jackson, Martin Van Buren, William Harrison, John Tyler, and James Polk—led the United States in the 20 years from 1829 to 1849. These were years of great growth for America. Also during this period, some of America's most important reform movements were begun and some of the country's greatest literature and art were produced. At the same time, however, the split between the North and the South widened. This split was caused by the unresolved issue of slavery.

## Land and People

There were 24 states in the Union in 1829. By 1849, there were 30 states. Arkansas became a state in 1836, and Michigan in 1837. Texas and Florida were annexed in 1845. Iowa was

*In 1849, Pittsburgh, Pennsylvania, was one of the large, thriving cities in America.*

annexed in 1846, and Wisconsin became a state in 1848. As a result, the total land area of the United States in 1849 was nearly 3 million square miles. That was more than three times what it had been in 1789, when the Constitution went into effect. In addition, the winning of the Mexican War (1846–1848) brought America a vast region from which the states of California and New Mexico, as well as Arizona, Colorado, Nevada, and Utah, would later be created.

America's population, too, had greatly increased. In 1789, the population was a little less than 4 million people. By 1849, it had increased almost six times, to about 23 million people. Most Americans still lived on farms. Only about 15 percent lived in cities, but that was a big increase from earlier times. In 1789, there were no cities in America with a population of more than 100,000 people. By 1849, there were five: New York City, New York; Philadelphia, Pennsylvania; Baltimore, Maryland; Boston, Massachusetts; and New Orleans, Louisiana.

The growth in the urban population was partly the result of immigration to the United States. Earlier in the 1800s, the rate of immigration was very low. But in the 1830s, about 500,000 people settled in America. In the 1840s, the number rose to 1.5 million. In 1850 alone, about 370,000 people came. The majority emigrated from Ireland, Germany, and Great Britain.

★ ★ ★ ★ ★ ★ ★ ★ ★ ★ ★ ★ ★ ★ ★ ★ ★ ★ ★ ★ ★ ★ ★ ★ ★ ★ ★

## *The Economy*

America's economy was also growing, but different regions were developing in different ways. The overall economy was based on agriculture, which would be the case until the end of the 1850s. But manufacturing was on the rise, especially in the North. Steam power, derived from the burning of coal, was replacing water power. The leading industries of the time were flour milling, iron production, and the manufacture of cotton textiles.

The South remained overwhelmingly agricultural. Cotton, tobacco, corn, and wheat were the main crops. Unlike the economies in other parts of the country, the South's economy was almost entirely dependent on slavery. This was so even though only one southern white family in four owned slaves. Still, most southerners could not imagine a society without slavery to support it. Consequently, the South was very sensitive to any movement that seemed hostile to slavery.

Both the North and the South continued to import (buy from other countries) more goods than it exported (sold to other countries). Textiles and iron products were the major imports. Cotton was the main export.

Gold was discovered in California in 1848, altering the economy of the West. A "gold rush" began as people traveled the long and difficult land and sea routes to the new territory, in the hopes of getting rich fast.

*The discovery of gold in California brought many people to the West.*

★ ★ ★ ★ ★ ★ ★ ★ ★ ★ ★ ★ ★ ★ ★ ★ ★ ★ ★ ★ ★ ★ ★ ★ ★

Both contributing to and resulting from economic growth was what historians call the transportation revolution. This was the great boom in the construction of roads, canals, and railroads that made moving people and goods from one place to another faster, easier, and cheaper. It has been estimated that in 1817, shipping goods from Cincinnati, Ohio, to New York City would have taken 52 days. After the opening of the Erie Canal (1825) and other canals, shipping the same goods took as few as 18 days. By the 1850s, shipping by railroad delivered goods to New York in about one week.

The Baltimore & Ohio Railroad had begun laying track as early as 1828, although the greatest spurt in railroad construction occurred in the 1850s. Following the 1848 California gold rush, some political leaders and businesspeople began devising a transcontinental rail system, which eventually spanned the country from the Atlantic Ocean to the Pacific Ocean.

Because most of the new transportation routes went from the Northeast to the West, they served to tie the West to the North much more than to the South. This contributed to the South's view of itself as a society separate and different from the rest of the country.

## Reformers, Writers, and Artists

In the years 1829 to 1849, important reform movements—attempts to change and improve American life—developed. Many of the people involved in these movements had strong religious beliefs about how to live moral lives. Reformers gave speeches, wrote books and articles, and formed organizations in attempts to persuade government at all levels to change certain laws. These movements had an enormous impact on the country.

One was the temperance movement, which sought to ban alcoholic beverages. The American Temperance Society was

★ ★ ★ ★ ★ ★ ★ ★ ★ ★ ★ ★ ★ ★ ★ ★ ★ ★ ★ ★ ★ ★ ★ ★ ★

## The Tragedy of the Native Americans

In the history of America, the growth and development of the United States as a whole often meant tragedy for the original inhabitants of the continent. These Native Americans, or American Indians, were pushed aside, often violently, to make room for the white settlers who wanted their land. The story of the Native Americans took a particularly tragic turn in the 1830s and 1840s.

In 1830, Congress passed the Indian Removal Act, which authorized the president to negotiate treaties with Native American tribes living east of the Mississippi River. In exchange for their lands, the tribes would be provided with land west of the Mississippi River—known as the Indian, or Oklahoma, Territory—and would be helped to move there. At the time, this was considered by the government to be a humane way of dealing with Native Americans.

For the Native Americans, however, it was a disaster. The tribes were tricked and cheated. Hunger, disease, and exposure to harsh weather killed many as they moved west in a series of journeys known as the Trail of Tears.

The Cherokee, Chickasaw, Choctaw, Creek, and Seminole peoples who had lived in the Southeast suffered especially. These tribes—called the Five Civilized Tribes by whites in the early 1800s—had lived in permanent settlements. They had established schools and legislatures. Historians have estimated that the Indian Removal Act cost the Cherokee a quarter of their population and the Creek two fifths of theirs. The Seminoles in Florida refused to move. The U.S. government waged a seven-year war, from 1835 to 1842, to force most of the Seminoles to move west.

founded in 1826. Several states passed laws prohibiting the sale of alcoholic beverages.

Another was the abolitionist movement, which sought to end slavery. Abolitionists believed that slavery was morally wrong and should be done away with as quickly as possible. Among the movement's leaders were William Lloyd Garrison, Wendell Phillips, and Frederick Douglass. Most of the abolitionists were northerners, but some southerners, such as the Grimké sisters of South Carolina, were also involved. They developed a network

## Notable Inventions

Several important American inventions of the 1830s and 1840s had a great impact on the quality of life in America. They included:

| | |
|---|---|
| 1831 | the reaper, invented by Cyrus H. McCormick |
| 1835 | the revolver, invented by Samuel Colt |
| 1837 | the steel plow, marketed by John Deere |
| 1844 | the telegraph, put into operation by Samuel F. B. Morse after he invented it in 1832 |
| 1846 | the sewing machine, invented by Elias Howe |
| 1849 | the safety pin, invented by Walter Hunt |

called the Underground Railroad to help runaway slaves. They also sent petitions to members of Congress, demanding the abolition of slavery. But for eight years, from 1836 to 1844, southern congressmen in the House of Representatives were able to rely on the "gag rule," a measure that had been adopted to prevent such petitions from being read.

In the late 1840s, a women's rights movement was formed. Elizabeth Cady Stanton, Lucretia Mott, and others sponsored a convention at the town of Seneca Falls, New York, in 1848. The convention adopted a Declaration of Sentiments that was modeled on the Declaration of Independence. It said, "We hold these truths to be self-evident: that all men and women are created equal." The Declaration of Sentiments went on to say that man had oppressed woman: "He has endeavored, in every way he could, to destroy her confidence in her own powers, to lessen her self-respect, and to make her willing to lead a dependent and abject life."

*Lucretia Mott*

Also active during these years were some of America's greatest thinkers and writers. Ralph Waldo Emerson and Henry David Thoreau were neighbors in Concord, Massachusetts. Poets and essayists, the two were also members of the Transcendental Club. Transcendentalism stressed the uniqueness of individual experience and the importance of self-reliance.

Nathaniel Hawthorne of Massachusetts and Herman Melville of New York began publishing fiction in the 1830s and 1840s, although their most well-known works came a little later. Edgar Allan Poe was born in Boston and grew up in Virginia. He wrote many gripping poems and stories before dying of alcoholism in 1849.

*Edgar Allan Poe*

Among the many important artists of the period were George Catlin and John James Audubon. Catlin is known especially for his paintings of Native Americans, and Audubon is famous for his studies of birds. Audubon also did pioneering work to protect the environment.

## The Growing Split Between the North and the South

Despite the country's economic, industrial, and artistic gains, however, many thoughtful people were troubled. They worried about the future of the Union. The North and the South—one a region with few slaves, the other a region whose whole economy was based on slavery—were increasingly at odds. Many disputes in Congress, for example, reflected differences between northern and southern senators and congressmen. Some leaders sought to avoid topics that in some way involved the question of slavery, such as the annexation of Texas. Still, the issue of slavery would not go away.

★ ★ ★ ★ ★ ★ ★ ★ ★ ★ ★ ★ ★ ★ ★ ★ ★ ★ ★ ★ ★ ★ ★ ★ ★ ★ ★ ★

Andrew Jackson
7th President of the United States

Term: *March 4, 1829–March 4, 1837; Democratic*
First Lady: *Rachel Donelson Robards Jackson*
Vice-Presidents: *John C. Calhoun and Martin Van Buren*

# 2

★  ★  ★

# Andrew Jackson

The man taking the oath of office as the seventh president of the United States on March 4, 1829, was tall and lean. He had a scar on his forehead from a British soldier's sword and carried in his body two bullets from duels he had fought. During one duel, in 1806, Jackson took a bullet near his heart. He remained standing and shot his opponent dead. Andrew Jackson was tough—which was one reason why the troops he had commanded years earlier gave him the nickname Old Hickory.

## *Early Life*

Andrew Jackson was born in South Carolina on March 15, 1767. He was the third son of Scottish-Irish immigrants who had come to America two years earlier. Andrew was named after his father, who died before he was born. He took after his strong-willed, self-reliant mother.

Young Andrew was given a good education, but he quit school to fight in the Revolutionary War. The British captured Andrew and his brother during the war. (Jackson was the only president to have been a prisoner of war.) When he refused to clean a British officer's boots, he received a sword cut that left a scar on his head. Andrew's two brothers died while serving in the army during the Revolution.

Jackson became a lawyer in 1787 and settled in Nashville, Tennessee. He married Rachel Donelson in 1791; he then "remarried" her in 1794 after learning that the first ceremony was not legally valid. Like many men on the frontier in his time, Jackson invested heavily in land with borrowed money. Some of his investments went bad. When the banks demanded their money, he nearly wound up in jail for debt. This gave him a life-long hatred of banks.

Jackson had a fiery temper. He was particularly sensitive to what he thought were insults to his or his wife's honor. As president, he sometimes even took advantage of his reputation for being bad tempered. To pressure someone, he might pretend to fly into a rage. The moment that person left, though, he would be in a perfectly good humor. His favorite diversions were horse racing and cockfighting. Jackson also liked to smoke pipes.

## *Enters Public Life*

In 1796, Jackson served in the convention that wrote Tennessee's first state constitution. He was elected to the House of Representatives in 1796, as a follower of Thomas Jefferson, and then served in the Senate and as a judge in Tennessee. The Jeffersonians, or followers of Jefferson, believed in interpreting the Constitution strictly. They were opposed to the Federalists, who followed John Adams and Alexander Hamilton. Jackson returned to the Senate in the 1820s.

★ ★ ★ ★ ★ ★ ★ ★ ★ ★ ★ ★ ★ ★ ★ ★ ★ ★ ★ ★ ★ ★ ★ ★ ★ ★ ★ ★

# First Lady Rachel Jackson

Andrew Jackson's beloved wife, Rachel, was born on June 15, 1767, in Virginia. She was exactly three months younger than him. Rachel's family later moved to Kentucky.

At 17, she married Lewis Robards. Rachel and Robards had a stormy marriage. For a while, they separated, and she returned to her family. Jackson met her while he was boarding with them.

Rachel and Lewis Robards lived together again briefly, but Robards asked for a divorce in 1790.

Thinking that the divorce had been completed, Rachel and Jackson married in August 1791. However, Lewis Robards had not completed the paperwork. Hearing of Rachel's "marriage" to Jackson, he sued for divorce, accusing her of adultery. The divorce was finally granted in 1793.

Rachel and Andrew Jackson "remarried" in January 1794. For the rest of his life, Jackson would go into a rage whenever anyone made remarks—as political opponents sometimes did—about his wife's honor or their marriage.

Always uncomfortable in Washington, Rachel Jackson had no desire to live in the White House. When her husband was elected president, she said, "I had rather be a door-keeper in the house of my Lord than live in that palace in Washington. For Mr. Jackson's sake, I am glad; for my own part, I never wished it."

*Rachel Donelson Robards Jackson*

She never did live in the White House. Long in poor health, Rachel Jackson died of a heart attack on December 22, 1828, little more than two months before her husband's inauguration. Jackson always blamed her death on the slanders made against them during the election campaign. At her funeral, he said, "In the presence of this dear saint, I can and do forgive all my enemies. But those vile wretches who have slandered her must look to God for mercy."

Rachel Jackson had no children from either of her marriages. But in 1809, she and Jackson adopted a nephew of hers. Nieces performed the duties of White House hostess during Jackson's presidency.

The Tennessee militia chose Jackson as their general in 1802, and ten years later, he became a general in the U.S. Army. Jackson's military career was both glorious and stormy. He defeated the Creek Indians in 1814. In 1815, he crushed the British at New Orleans in the War of 1812 and became a national hero. In 1818, he chased the Seminole Indians across the U.S. border into Spanish Florida. There, without authorization, he executed two British citizens.

His actions in Florida provoked much controversy. Secretary of War John C. Calhoun disapproved, and Jackson and Calhoun later became enemies. Other leaders also questioned Jackson's judgment. Former president Thomas Jefferson, for one, said, "I feel very much alarmed at the prospect of seeing General Jackson president. He is one of the most unfit men I know of for the place. . . . He is a dangerous man."

Nonetheless, the Tennessee legislature nominated Jackson to run for president in 1824. It was an unusual election because there were three other candidates: John Quincy Adams of Massachusetts, Secretary of the Treasury William H. Crawford of Georgia, and Speaker of the House of Representatives Henry Clay

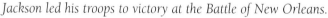

*Jackson led his troops to victory at the Battle of New Orleans.*

of Kentucky. At first, Calhoun was also a candidate, but he later announced that he would settle for the vice-presidency, with either Adams or Jackson.

By this time, the old Federalist party had just about disappeared. Jefferson's Democratic-Republican party was splitting into various factions. The four candidates represented the different regions of the country more than they did anything else. Adams was strongest in the Northeast, and Crawford prevailed in the South. Clay and Jackson divided the West.

The 1824 election results were not decisive. Calhoun was elected vice-president, but not one of the presidential candidates won the required majority. Jackson won 99 electoral votes, Adams 84, Crawford 41, and Clay 37. When no one has a majority, the Constitution provides that the president be chosen by the House of Representatives, voting by state, from among the three candidates with the most electoral votes. With the fewest votes, Clay was eliminated, so he had to decide whom to support.

Clay chose to back Adams. That helped Adams win the votes of a majority of states in the House and thus become president. When Adams announced that he was appointing Clay secretary of state, supporters of the other candidates were outraged. Jackson's followers, in particular, accused Adams and Clay of making a "corrupt bargain." Although there is no evidence that Adams had promised the post to Clay for his support, Jackson supporters made an issue of it.

## The Election of 1828—A Landmark in American History

In 1828, Jackson ran again. The Democratic-Republican party had now split up. One part, called the Democrats, chose Jackson as its candidate for president and Calhoun for vice-president. The other, the National Republicans (many of whom would become

★ ★ ★ ★ ★ ★ ★ ★ ★ ★ ★ ★ ★ ★ ★ ★ ★ ★ ★ ★ ★ ★ ★ ★ ★ ★ ★ ★

Whigs in the 1830s), supported the re-election of Adams and Richard Rush of Pennsylvania for vice-president.

Jackson had come to represent a new force in American politics. He was the candidate of western frontiersmen, southern farmers, and northern workers. For many, he was a hero. He was thought to represent the interests of middle-class people as opposed to those of wealthy bankers, owners of great plantations, and others who enjoyed special privileges.

In 1828, more people than ever before were eligible to vote. States were abolishing their property and religious qualifications for voting. Nearly every white man could vote if he wanted to. (Women and, in many places, free black men, however, still could not vote; nor could slaves.)

The election that year was also notable in another way. Presidents are actually elected by electoral votes cast by members of the Electoral College. Every state has as many electoral votes as it has senators and congressmen. Each state decides for itself how its members of the Electoral College are chosen. In the early years of the country's history, most of the state legislatures chose the members of the Electoral College. By 1828, however, all but two states (Delaware and South Carolina) were choosing them by popular vote—the votes of the people. On Election Day, then, voters were technically voting for members of the Electoral College. In actuality, though, they were voting for a presidential candidate, because those running for election to

*Jackson was a popular candidate among the middle class.*

the Electoral College were pledged to cast electoral votes for particular candidates. (This same procedure is followed today.) So there developed a significant popular vote for the president.

The 1828 campaign itself featured absurd personal attacks by both sides. Jackson was called a madman, a murderer, and an adulterer. Adams was criticized in equally outrageous ways and for making the "corrupt" bargain with Clay.

Jackson won the election. He received almost 650,000 popular votes and 178 electoral votes. Adams got a little more than 500,000 popular votes and only 83 electoral votes. Jackson won all the states south of Pennsylvania and west of New Jersey, as well as half of New York's electoral votes. Old Hickory was going to the White House, with Calhoun as his vice-president.

*John C. Calhoun was vice-president during Jackson's first term.*

## Jackson as President

Jackson believed that the president was the "direct representative of the American people" and was "responsible to them." If Congress passed bills he did not like, he vetoed them. Previous presidents had used their veto power only if they thought a proposed law was unconstitutional. Jackson vetoed 12 bills, more than all his predecessors together.

According to Jackson, any decent citizen could serve in the government. He said, "The duties of all public officers are so plain and simple that men of intelligence may readily qualify themselves for their performance." There should be rotation in office as well: Individuals, he felt, should not stay in public posts for many years because they tended to become corrupt. In the 1828 campaign, Jackson had pledged to sweep the "corrupt" opposition out of office.

★ ★ ★ ★ ★ ★ ★ ★ ★ ★ ★ ★ ★ ★ ★ ★ ★ ★ ★ ★ ★ ★ ★ ★

These views and his loyalty to his supporters led to the practice, after an election, of removing from office members of the opposing political party and replacing them with members of the winning party. When he got to the White House, Jackson removed from the federal government nearly 1,000 employees in favor of people from among his supporters. Replying to criticisms of Jackson's policy, Senator William L. Marcy, a Democrat from New York, said, "to the victor belong the spoils of the enemy." Thus, such practices became known as the spoils system.

Actually, Jackson's action was not all that new. The system had long been practiced in state governments. And in 1800, when Jefferson and his party had come to power after years of rule by the Federalists, they had removed many Federalists from office. Jefferson and Jackson removed about the same proportion—one fifth—of officeholders.

Jackson's vigorous assertion of the powers of the presidency provoked much criticism. Opponents tried to ridicule him by calling him King Andrew. That criticism led to the name of the political party that formed to oppose Jackson: the Whig party. Whig was a name taken from English history. At the time of the

## The Masses Come to the White House

The day Jackson was inaugurated, Washington, D.C., witnessed a scene that it had never before experienced. Thousands of people had come to town to see their hero sworn in as president.

At the end of the ceremony at the Capitol building, the new president bent low in a bow to the crowd of people. Delighted, many of them then headed for the White House, where there was to be a reception.

No one was prepared for what happened next. A large crowd stormed through the doors. In a frenzy, they broke fine china, stood on the furniture, and jumped through windows. Jackson had to be ushered by friends out a side door to avoid being crushed!

English Civil War in the 1600s, the Whigs were the political group seeking to limit the power of the king.

In the United States, the Whig party formed in the early 1830s, during Jackson's second term. The Whigs criticized what they viewed as Jackson's abuse of presidential power. They also favored a national bank and federal aid for internal improvements—roads, canals, and, later, railroads—as well as a high tariff tax on imports—to support economic growth. They tended to dislike such immigrant groups as the Irish Catholics. Some were against slavery.

*As shown in this political cartoon, Jackson was called King Andrew by the Whigs.*

## The Nullification Crisis

One of the major issues of Jackson's presidency concerned nullification. Nullification was the idea that a state could nullify, or make invalid, a federal law within its borders. It was an extreme version of states' rights—the belief that the powers of the states needed to be protected and that it was dangerous for the federal government to gain power. Supporters of states' rights believed that if the federal government got stronger, it would threaten the liberty of the people. Southerners were most concerned about states' rights. Some of them feared that, ultimately, the federal government might threaten slavery.

The issue arose in connection with a tariff law. Many southerners opposed high tariffs because they thought the tariffs might raise prices for imports and reduce the sale of their farm products in other countries. People in South Carolina were particularly concerned about tariffs. In 1828, Congress passed a high tariff

★ ★ ★ ★ ★ ★ ★ ★ ★ ★ ★ ★ ★ ★ ★ ★ ★ ★ ★ ★ ★ ★ ★ ★ ★ ★ ★

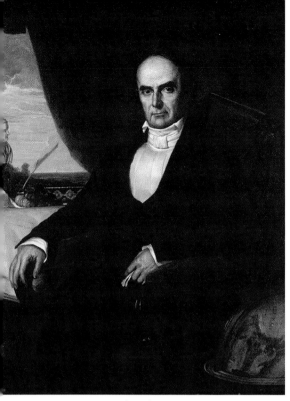
*Senator Daniel Webster*

that South Carolina had bitterly opposed. Vice-President Calhoun, a South Carolinian, had written an article against the law. In it, he claimed that a state could nullify a law it did not like.

A famous debate took place in Congress in 1830 over nullification and states' rights. Senator Robert Hayne of South Carolina said that a state's power to nullify was essential to preserving freedom. In reply, Senator Daniel Webster of Massachusetts stated that nullification would destroy the Union. Webster ended his speech with "Liberty and Union, now and forever, one and inseparable!" At a dinner shortly afterward, the president seemed to side with Webster. Jackson offered a toast: "Our Federal Union. It must be preserved." Calhoun responded, "The Union, next to our liberty, the most dear."

The issue continued unresolved until Congress lowered the tariff a little, in 1832. The people of South Carolina, however, still objected to it, and they elected a special convention to discuss the state's position. The convention called the tariff law "null, void, and no law." The convention further stated that if the federal government tried to enforce the law, South Carolina would secede, or withdraw from, the Union.

Jackson issued a proclamation saying that secession was treason. He promised to enforce the law and urged South Carolina to obey it. He warned South Carolinians that "if one drop of blood be shed there in defiance of the laws of the United States, I will hang the first man of them I can get my hands on to the first tree I can find." Jackson asked Congress to pass a Force Bill, which would give him authority to use the army to enforce the tariff law if necessary.

★ ★ ★ ★ ★ ★ ★ ★ ★ ★ ★ ★ ★ ★ ★ ★ ★ ★ ★ ★ ★ ★ ★ ★ ★ ★ ★

Senator Henry Clay of Kentucky worked out a compromise. A new tariff was passed, further lowering the rates. Calhoun, who had resigned as vice-president to become a senator from South Carolina, said that the new rates were acceptable. The Force Bill was also passed, and South Carolina withdrew its secession threat. Jackson said, "Nullification is dead." But he predicted, correctly, that the next reason for secession would be the slavery question.

## Jackson Fights the U.S. Bank and Is Re-elected

The Second Bank of the United States had been chartered by Congress in 1816. The Bank alone handled the government's finances, and it had greatly helped the American economy in the 1820s. But it was owned and run by wealthy bankers in the East. Jackson and others hated the Bank for a variety of reasons. One reason was that the Bank followed policies of raising the cost of loans, which took advantage of farmers in the South and the West, who often needed to borrow money. Another was that it took business away from state banks. Some supporters of states' rights considered the Bank to be unconstitutional.

The Bank's charter permitting it to operate was not due to expire until 1836, but Jackson made clear shortly after becoming president that he opposed renewing it. Alarmed, the director of the Bank, Nicholas Biddle, and his ally, Senator Henry Clay, decided to press for renewal early. Jackson said, "The Bank is trying to kill me, *but I will kill it.*" And he did.

Congress passed a renewal bill in July 1832. Jackson vetoed it. He claimed that the Bank was a dangerously powerful private organization. "When the laws undertake to . . . make the rich richer and the potent more powerful, the humble members of society . . . have a right to complain of the injustice of their government." The Bank's charter expired in March 1836.

★  ★  ★  ★  ★  ★  ★  ★  ★  ★  ★  ★  ★  ★  ★  ★  ★  ★  ★  ★  ★  ★  ★  ★  ★

*Martin Van Buren was vice-president during Jackson's second term.*

In the 1832 election, the National Republicans nominated Henry Clay to run for president and John Sergeant of Pennsylvania to run for vice-president. The Democrats renominated Jackson and chose Martin Van Buren of New York as their vice-presidential candidate. A third party, the Anti-Masons, had formed to oppose secret societies and Jackson. It nominated William Wirt of Maryland and Amos Ellmaker of Pennsylvania. Jackson's vetoes, the spoils system, and, above all, the Bank were the major issues of the campaign. The election was a triumph for Jackson.

At the start of his second term, Jackson removed federal money from the U.S. Bank and had it deposited in state banks. The Senate criticized him for exceeding his authority, but he ignored it. The state banks then unwisely issued large amounts of paper money, without having enough gold and silver, called specie, to back it. The easy availability of all this money caused a huge rush to buy public and other lands. Eventually, near the end of his term, Jackson had to issue a policy called the Specie Circular. It required buyers of federal land to pay in gold or silver. The land-buying boom ended, and a financial panic erupted in 1837 as people tried to convert paper money to specie and the banks did not have enough specie to meet the demand.

*An 1837 political cartoon satirized Jackson's war on the U.S. Bank and the Panic of 1837.*

# Third Parties and the First Nominating Conventions

During most of America's history, there have been two major political parties. From time to time, however, so-called third parties have formed and put forward presidential candidates. Sometimes, a third party has contributed valuable ideas. Occasionally, it has gone on to displace one of the two major parties.

In 1832, the Anti-Mason party opposed Jackson's re-election. It took votes away from Jackson's main opponent, the Republican Henry Clay, but it probably did not affect the outcome of the election.

A third party did, however, affect the outcome of the 1844 election. The anti-slavery Liberty party, founded in 1839, took enough votes in New York from Clay, now the Whig candidate, to enable Democrat James K. Polk to win the state. Polk narrowly won the election. Had Clay carried New York, he would have been elected.

Other parties taking strong anti-slavery stands followed in the 1840s and 1850s. In 1848, the Free-Soil party helped elect Whig candidate Zachary Taylor and defeat Democrat Lewis Cass. One third party, the Republicans, became one of the two major parties—it still is today—and in 1860, elected Abraham Lincoln president.

In 1831, the Anti-Masons became the first party to hold a nominating convention to select its presidential and vice-presidential candidates. Previously, parties had usually chosen their candidates at meetings, called caucuses, of their congressional leaders. Caucuses came to be seen as undemocratic procedures. At a nominating convention, delegates chosen locally from all over the country get together and vote to select the party's candidates. Ever since the 1832 election, parties have held such conventions to pick their candidates.

## *After the White House*

When his second term ended, Jackson retired to his home, the Hermitage, near Nashville, Tennessee. He supported his successor, Martin Van Buren, and later James K. Polk, another Tennessean, who became president in 1845. He fell into debt—his policies as president had hurt his own finances—and suffered from tuberculosis, edema, cataracts, and other ailments. He died on June 8, 1845. Jackson's last words were, "Oh, do not cry. Be good children, and we shall all meet in Heaven."

★ ★ ★ ★ ★ ★ ★ ★ ★ ★ ★ ★ ★ ★ ★ ★ ★ ★ ★ ★ ★ ★ ★ ★ ★

Martin Van Buren
8th President of the United States

Term: *March 4, 1837–March 4, 1841; Democratic*
White House Hostess: *Angelica Singleton Van Buren*
Vice-President: *Richard M. Johnson*

# 3

★ ★ ★

# Martin Van Buren

M artin Van Buren followed Andrew Jackson as president. A loyal supporter of Jackson, Van Buren was totally unlike Old Hickory in most respects. He was a short, dignified man. Van Buren was a master politician. He often worked behind the scenes to make alliances and deals. For this, he acquired two nicknames in his political life: the Little Magician and the Red Fox of Kinderhook.

Van Buren lacked Jackson's tremendous popular appeal. When he was sworn in as president on March 4, 1837, his inaugural address was respectfully received, in contrast to Jackson's huge ovation. Senator Thomas Hart Benton commented, "For once, the rising sun was eclipsed by the setting sun."

## Early Life and Career

Van Buren was born in Kinderhook, New York, on December 5, 1782. He was the first president to be born after American independence was declared in 1776.

Van Buren became a lawyer and quickly entered politics as a Jeffersonian. Elected to New York's state senate in 1812, he joined a group known as the Albany Regency. It was highly influential in both state and national politics. Van Buren was elected to the Senate in 1820. He worked to strengthen the alliance between northern farmers and laborers and southern planters that was the base of the Democratic-Republican party.

Van Buren was elected governor of New York in 1828, but Jackson appointed him secretary of state in 1829. Later in his first term, Jackson wanted to appoint Van Buren minister to Britain, but the Senate rejected the appointment. Vice-President John C. Calhoun cast the deciding vote against Van Buren.

In 1832, Van Buren was elected vice-president, succeeding Calhoun. Four years later, the Democrats would nominate him, with Jackson's full support, to run for president. Richard M. Johnson of Kentucky was nominated to run for vice-president.

## The Election of 1836

The Whigs were not well organized enough to agree on a single presidential candidate. Instead, they put up different candidates in different regions, hoping to prevent Van Buren from getting a majority of electoral votes. That would force the election into the House of Representatives, as had happened in 1824. The Whigs ran William H. Harrison of Ohio, Daniel Webster of Massachusetts, and other candidates. They also ran various people for vice-president.

*Vice-President
Richard M. Johnson*

The campaign was mainly a judgment of Jackson. Van Buren said that he would "tread generally in the footsteps of President Jackson." The Whig strategy failed. Van Buren got 51 percent of the popular vote and 170 electoral votes, which was a majority.

★ ★ ★ ★ ★ ★ ★ ★ ★ ★ ★ ★ ★ ★ ★ ★ ★ ★ ★ ★ ★ ★ ★ ★ ★ ★ ★ ★

## The Widower President and His Four Sons

Martin Van Buren married Hannah Hoes in 1807, when he was 24 and she was 23. Like him, Hannah was of Dutch descent. Hannah died of tuberculosis in 1819.

The couple had four sons. The eldest son was named Abraham. He married Angelica Singleton in 1838, after they were introduced by Dolley Madison, the widow of former president James Madison. Angelica served as the White House hostess during Van Buren's presidency.

John, the second son, was a lawyer and became a congressman in 1841. He was a prominent abolitionist and did not believe that any compromise was reasonable on the issue of slavery. The younger sons, Martin and Smith Thompson, both served as aides to their father. Martin died while touring Europe with his father in 1855.

Van Buren never remarried. In the 1820s, it was rumored that he was

*Angelica Singleton Van Buren*

courting Ellen Randolph, a granddaughter of Thomas Jefferson. In 1851, when he was 68, he proposed to Margaret Sylvester, then 40. She was the daughter of the teacher with whom Van Buren had studied law. She declined his proposal, saying that she preferred to remain single.

No vice-presidential candidate got a majority of electoral votes, however. So, for the first and only time in American history, the Senate had to choose the vice-president. In February 1837, the Senate elected Johnson over Francis Granger of New York, 33 to 16.

## Van Buren as President

The state of the economy was the major problem of Van Buren's presidency. Just as his term as president was beginning, the Panic of 1837 was hitting the country. Throughout the United States, banks failed, people and businesses could not pay their debts, and workers lost their jobs. The price of cotton on the

New Orleans market fell to nearly half of what it had been. In New York, unemployed people, unable to buy food, rioted.

Van Buren took a popular stand when he said, "The less government interferes with private pursuits the better for the general prosperity." He did establish a maximum ten-hour workday for federal employees in 1840. But for the most part, Van Buren's proposals for the economy concerned ways to improve the nation's banking and money system. He insisted that payments to the government be in specie, not paper money. He proposed that Congress create an Independent Treasury in which federal money would be stored until needed. This was to avoid depositing the money in unsafe state banks or creating another privately owned national bank. The Independent Treasury proposal was opposed by the Whigs and did not pass until 1840. For most of his administration, the economy remained bad, and his popularity suffered.

Van Buren had more success in foreign affairs. In 1838, he effectively controlled a group of Americans threatening to use force to overthrow British rule in Canada. The next year, Van Buren prevented a war with Britain over a logging dispute along the Maine–New Brunswick, Canada, border.

Texas had won its independence from Mexico in 1836. It applied in 1837 for admission to the Union as a state. As Texas permitted slavery, however, its possible admittance threatened to revive unresolved differences between North and South. For this reason, Van Buren opposed admitting Texas to the Union. The position cost him the South's support in the next election.

## *Defeated at Re-election, Van Buren Remains Active in Politics*

In 1840, the Democrats renominated Van Buren for president. Vice-President Johnson was unpopular, however, in part because he had a common-law wife who was a former slave and they

★ ★ ★ ★ ★ ★ ★ ★ ★ ★ ★ ★ ★ ★ ★ ★ ★ ★ ★ ★ ★ ★ ★ ★ ★ ★ ★

raised their children as free persons. The Democrats nominated no one for vice-president.

The Whigs chose William H. Harrison and John Tyler. Van Buren was defeated in the election. Still, he remained active in public life. He toured the South in 1842, trying to build support for another run for the presidency. But his opposition to the annexation of Texas cost him the Democratic nomination in 1844. President Polk asked Van Buren to serve as minister to Britain, but he turned down the post.

*In 1848, Van Buren tried to regain the White House as a Free-Soil candidate. He was not successful.*

By 1848, Van Buren was taking the "free-soil" position, which opposed allowing slavery in territories that were not yet states. That year, the Free-Soil party nominated him to run for president. The party's slogan was "Free soil, free speech, and free men." Van Buren got no electoral votes, but he took enough votes away from Democrat Lewis Cass in New York State to enable Whig Zachary Taylor to win the state and the election.

In the following years, Van Buren returned to the Democratic party and favored compromise on the slavery question in the interest of preserving the Union. He retired to his home near Kinderhook and later traveled to Europe, where he met with Britain's Queen Victoria and Pope Pius IX. In addition, Van Buren wrote his autobiography and a history of American political parties. Looking back on his presidency, he wrote, "The two happiest days of [my] life were those of [my] entrance upon the office and of [my] surrender of it." Van Buren supported the North in the Civil War. He died on July 24, 1862.

★ ★ ★ ★ ★ ★ ★ ★ ★ ★ ★ ★ ★ ★ ★ ★ ★ ★ ★ ★ ★ ★ ★ ★ ★ ★ ★

William H. Harrison
9th President of the United States

Term: *March 4, 1841–April 4, 1841; Whig*
First Lady: *Anna Tuthill Symmes Harrison*
Vice-President: *John Tyler*

# 4

★  ★  ★

# William H. Harrison

W illiam Henry Harrison's presidency was noteworthy
in several respects.  At 68, Harrison was at the time
the oldest man to become president.  (Ronald Reagan
later became the oldest at 69, in 1980.)  Harrison was also the
first to die in office.  He was the first Whig party candidate to be
elected.  He gave the longest inaugural address on record—more
than one and a half hours.  And his presidency was the shortest
in American history—he died just one month after taking office.

## Harrison's Life and Early Career

William Henry Harrison was born in Virginia on February 9, 1773.
His father, Benjamin Harrison, had been one of the signers of the
Declaration of Independence.

A slender man of average height, Harrison at first studied to be a doctor.  But he joined the army in 1791 and had a successful military career.  He won a famous battle against the Shawnee Indians at Tippecanoe Creek in 1811.  In the War of 1812, Harrison defeated the British at the Battle of the Thames. Tecumseh, a great Indian chief and ally of the British, was killed in that battle.

President John Adams appointed Harrison the first governor of the Indiana Territory in 1800.  He served in Congress as a representative from Ohio from 1816 to 1819, and was elected to the Senate in 1824.  Harrison became a supporter of Henry Clay. In 1828, when Clay was secretary of state, Harrison was appointed minister to Colombia, but Jackson's election as president that year ended Harrison's diplomatic career.

*Harrison won a decisive battle against the Shawnee at Tippecanoe Creek.*

★  ★  ★  ★  ★  ★  ★  ★  ★  ★  ★  ★  ★  ★  ★  ★  ★  ★  ★  ★  ★  ★  ★  ★  ★

## First Lady Anna Harrison

William Henry Harrison married Anna Tuthill Symmes on November 25, 1795. Her father, John Cleves Symmes, had been chief justice of the New Jersey Supreme Court, but he had moved west and become a wealthy landowner in the Cincinnati area. Anna's father did not approve of her relationship with Harrison, and the couple eloped.

The Harrisons had ten children— six sons and four daughters. All but one son lived to maturity, but four sons and one daughter died before their father did, and one daughter died shortly afterward. The third son, John Scott Harrison, became a Whig congressman in the 1850s. Benjamin, one of John Scott's children with his second wife, became the 23rd president of the United States in 1889.

Anna Harrison did not go with her husband to Washington for his

*Anna Tuthill Symmes Harrison*

inauguration. She intended to move there in the spring of 1841. But as Harrison died on April 5, she never did. Thus, she never actually served as First Lady. Anna Harrison lived on in North Bend, Ohio, until her death on February 25, 1864, at the age of 88.

Because Harrison was a military hero, the Whigs thought he would make a strong presidential candidate. In 1836, they chose him as one of their regional candidates to run against Van Buren. He did the best of the group, winning more than half a million popular votes and 73 electoral votes. Four years later, Harrison actively sought the Whig nomination.

## The Election of 1840—"Tippecanoe and Tyler Too!"

When the Democrats renominated Martin Van Buren in 1840, they stated their positions on several major issues. The Democrats supported states' rights and opposed a national bank, internal improvements made at federal expense, and congressional interference in slavery.

Because the poor state of the economy had made President Van Buren unpopular, the Whigs thought that they had a strong chance to win in 1840.  They were determined not to offend anyone, so they avoided talking about the issues and chose a candidate they believed would appeal to all parts of the nation: Harrison.  For vice-president, the Whigs nominated John Tyler, a former Democrat, to appeal to southerners and other supporters of states' rights.

The campaign was unlike anything the nation had ever seen before.  Aware that hundreds of thousands of people were now voting, the Whigs worked hard to make Harrison into a popular hero in the mold of Jackson.  Rallies, floats, campaign hats, and other advertising devices were used to create a lot of enthusiasm

*The Whigs used parades and floats to promote Harrison's popularity.*

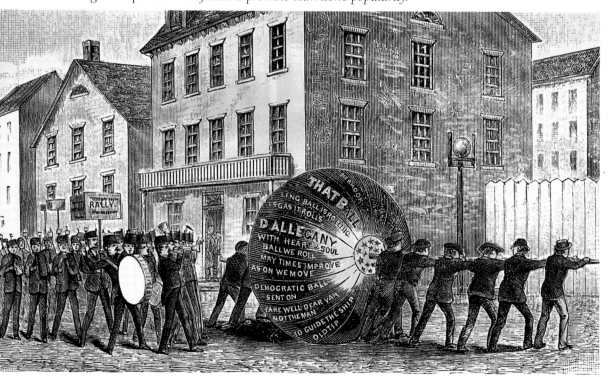

for Harrison. He was portrayed as a simple farmer who lived in a log cabin and drank hard cider, though in truth, Harrison lived in a 22-room mansion. A campaign song called "Tippecanoe and Tyler too!" referred to Harrison's fine war record and the vice-presidential nominee. One line of the song went, "Van, Van, is a used-up man."

The Whig effort succeeded. A record number of people voted, and 53 percent of them voted for Harrison and Tyler. Harrison got 234 electoral votes; Van Buren received only 60. Even New York, Van Buren's home state, and Tennessee, where Jackson supported him, went against him. The Whigs also won control of both houses of Congress.

## The Shortest Presidency

March 4, 1841, was a windy, raw day. Nevertheless, Harrison delivered his inaugural address without wearing a coat, hat, or gloves. A few days later, he was drenched in a cold rainstorm.

Harrison quickly named his Cabinet. It was headed by Daniel Webster as secretary of state. Most of the others were followers of Henry Clay. But, worn down by the chores of making other appointments, the president fell ill and died of pneumonia on April 4, 1841.

Never before had a president died in office. The Constitution says that in such a situation, the "Powers and Duties" of the office "shall devolve" on the vice-president. Did that mean that the vice-president became the president? John Tyler and the Cabinet at first disagreed. The Cabinet maintained that Tyler was just "Vice President, Acting President." Tyler insisted that he was president, and he refused to open mail addressed to the "Acting President." Eventually, Tyler prevailed, and in May, Congress formally recognized him as president. The precedent that he set has been followed ever since.

★ ★ ★ ★ ★ ★ ★ ★ ★ ★ ★ ★ ★ ★ ★ ★ ★ ★ ★ ★ ★ ★ ★ ★ ★ ★ ★

John Tyler
10th President of the United States

Term: *April 4, 1841–March 4, 1845; Whig*
First Ladies: *Letitia Christian Tyler and Julia Gardiner Tyler*
Vice-President: *None*

# 5

★ ★ ★

# John Tyler

T yler's presidency, like Harrison's, was also unusual. For one thing, it was not completely clear whether he really was president. He antagonized both political parties and was almost continuously at war with Congress. At 51, he was the youngest president up to that time. He had more children than any other president and was the first both to become a widower and to remarry while in office.

## Tyler's Early Life and Career

John Tyler was born on March 29, 1790, in Virginia. Tyler was named after his father, who was a moderately wealthy planter and a friend of Thomas Jefferson. John Tyler's mother died when he was seven. His father and Harrison's father knew each other and, at times, were political rivals.

Tyler graduated from William and Mary College and became a lawyer. When he was 21, he won a seat in the Virginia legislature. Later, he served in the House of Representatives, as governor of Virginia, and in the Senate. Tyler believed in states' rights. Although he was a Democrat and at first supported Jackson, he broke with Jackson over the Force Bill and other issues. Tyler thought Jackson was abusing his authority. Showing the stubbornness that he would often display as president, Tyler resigned from the Senate rather than change his vote criticizing Jackson in 1836, as the Virginia legislature had instructed.

The Whigs thought they could use Tyler to gain votes among the supporters of states' rights. In 1836, he ran in some states as the vice-presidential candidate.

## Tyler's Problems and Accomplishments

More difficult problems lay ahead. The Democrats would not help Tyler because he had broken with them and helped defeat them. But Tyler was not really a Whig, either. He was against a national bank, internal improvements, and high tariffs—which the Whigs favored; and he supported states' rights—which the Whigs were against. He disagreed with the Cabinet, which was composed of Whigs, and the Congress, which was dominated by them. Just about the only thing that they had agreed on was the Constitution's intention to make Congress more powerful than the president. But now Tyler, a man who liked being his own boss, was the president!

The Whigs, of course, were not happy, either. After Harrison was elected, they had expected to carry out their program. Now Tyler stood in their way and vetoed many of their proposals. Referring to Tyler, the great Whig leader Henry Clay said, "If a God-directed thunderbolt were to strike and annihilate the traitor, all would say that 'Heaven is just.'"

★ ★ ★ ★ ★ ★ ★ ★ ★ ★ ★ ★ ★ ★ ★ ★ ★ ★ ★ ★ ★ ★ ★ ★

# A First Lady Dies and a President Remarries

In 1813, while serving in the Virginia House of Delegates, John Tyler married Letitia Christian. She was the daughter of a well-off planter. Their courtship had lasted five years. A few months before their wedding, Tyler wrote to her, "Whether I float or sink in the stream of fortune, you may be assured of this, that I shall never cease to love you."

*Letitia Christian Tyler*

The couple had eight children, seven of whom lived to adulthood. Letitia Tyler suffered a paralyzing stroke in 1839. While in the White House as First Lady, she came downstairs from her living quarters only once. That was to attend the wedding of the couple's daughter Elizabeth in January 1842. Their daughter-in-law, the actress Priscilla Cooper Tyler, was the hostess for White House social functions. Letitia Tyler died on September 10, 1842.

*Julia Gardiner Tyler*

Earlier that year, Tyler had met 22-year-old Julia Gardiner at a White House reception. Her father was a wealthy New York State landowner and state senator. After Letitia Tyler's death, the two began seeing each other. The president proposed in early 1843, but at first Julia declined.

On February 28, 1844, the couple was involved in a disaster that killed Julia's father, two Cabinet officers, and several others. The group was sailing down the Potomac River on a new warship. When one of the ship's guns was fired, it exploded. Tyler and Julia were spared because they were below deck at that moment.

Tyler persisted with his courtship, and Julia changed her mind. They were married quietly in New York City on June 26, 1844. Tyler's daughters were not happy about their father's remarriage. His eldest, Mary, was five years older than her new stepmother.

John and Julia Tyler had seven children. The youngest, Pearl Tyler, was born in 1860, when her father was 70, and lived until 1947.

Julia Tyler enjoyed being First Lady and gave grand parties in the White House. She started the custom of having a band play "Hail to the Chief" when the president appears. She survived her husband by 27 years. On July 10, 1889, she died in Richmond, Virginia.

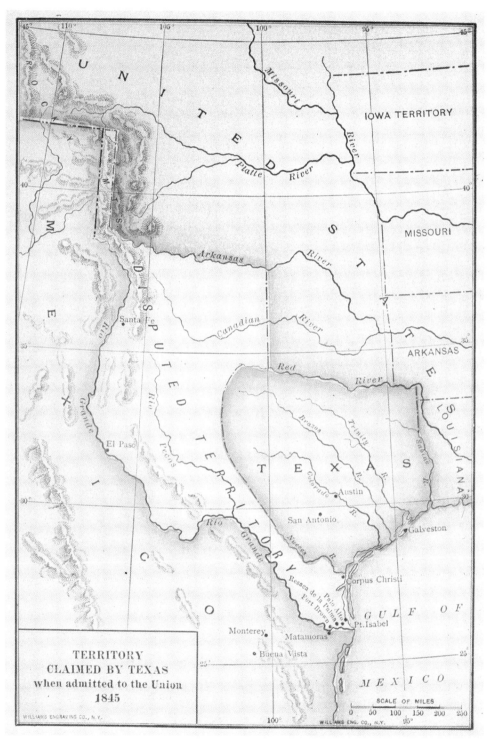

TERRITORY
CLAIMED BY TEXAS
when admitted to the Union
1845

*The annexation of Texas added a huge amount of territory to the Union.*

★ ★ ★ ★ ★ ★ ★ ★ ★ ★ ★ ★ ★ ★ ★ ★ ★ ★ ★ ★ ★ ★ ★ ★ ★ ★ ★ ★ ★

The result was constant arguing. At one point, the entire Cabinet, except for Secretary of State Webster, resigned. In less than four years, the six Cabinet posts were occupied by 19 different men. One day, Tyler nominated Caleb Cushing to be secretary of the treasury three times, and the Senate rejected him each time!

Tyler did have some successes. The Webster-Ashburton Treaty of 1842 with Britain settled disputed portions of the boundary between the United States and Canada. It also provided for joint efforts to stop the slave trade.

Tyler also brought about the annexation of Texas. He made a treaty with Texas in 1844, but because it got caught up in a dispute about slavery, the Senate refused to ratify (approve) it. However, after James K. Polk, who favored annexation, won the presidential election of 1844, Congress approved the annexation by passing a joint resolution that Tyler signed. Texas officially joined the Union at the end of 1845.

## *After the White House*

Tyler considered running for president in 1845. But no party would support him, and he did not want to cause the Democratic candidate, James K. Polk, to lose to the Whig candidate, Henry Clay. So he retired to his estate near Richmond, Virginia, and devoted himself to his family. He rejoined the Democratic party and also became the head of William and Mary College.

In February 1861, Tyler chaired a convention in Washington, D.C., that tried to work out a compromise between the North and the South. But the attempt failed, and Tyler supported Virginia when it seceded from the Union in April. Later that year, John Tyler was elected to the Confederate Congress. Before he could actually participate in the Congress, though, he died, on January 18, 1862.

★ ★ ★ ★ ★ ★ ★ ★ ★ ★ ★ ★ ★ ★ ★ ★ ★ ★ ★ ★ ★ ★ ★ ★

James K. Polk
11th President of the United States

Term: *March 4, 1845–March 4, 1849; Democratic*
First Lady: *Sarah Childress Polk*
Vice-President: *George M. Dallas*

# 6

★ ★ ★

# James K. Polk

James Knox Polk is not one of the most famous presidents. Yet his policies changed the United States in very important ways. Polk served only one term, but that was his choice. He set his goals, and he accomplished them. George Bancroft, a historian who served as Polk's secretary of the navy, said that Polk was "one of the very foremost of our public men, and one of the very best and most honest and most successful Presidents the country ever had."

## Early Years

James K. Polk was born on November 2, 1795, in Mecklenburg County, North Carolina. His family was of Scottish-Irish descent. The family moved to Tennessee in 1806, where James's father became rich from buying and selling land.

As a child, Polk was not very healthy. When he was 17, he underwent surgery to have his gallstones removed—at a time when anesthesia was unknown! Polk grew into a solidly built man of average height. All his life, however, he worked himself too hard. An excellent student, he graduated first in his class at the University of North Carolina in 1818.

Polk became a lawyer. He was elected to the Tennessee legislature in 1823. There he became a close follower of Andrew Jackson; people sometimes jokingly called him Young Hickory. In 1825, he was elected to the House of Representatives. He was re-elected six times and was speaker of the House from 1835 to 1839. Polk was the only speaker to become president.

Polk was elected governor of Tennessee in 1839 but lost a re-election bid in 1841 and again in 1843. While governor, he usually avoided lavish social affairs. He said that he "could not lose half a day just to go and dine."

## The Election of 1844

Polk was considered likely to get the vice-presidential nomination at the Democratic Convention in 1844. Former president Martin Van Buren was the favorite for president. Van Buren, however, had lost support from southern and western delegates because he continued to oppose the annexation of Texas. After eight ballots, the convention still had not chosen a nominee. Polk had announced that he supported adding Texas and the Oregon Territory to the Union. His position was that both areas had always belonged to the United States. On the ninth ballot, Polk won the nomination. Polk was the first "dark horse" (successful candidate not expected to win) nominee in American history. He had never been thought of as a serious contender. Polk immediately declared that he would serve only one term if elected. George M. Dallas of Pennsylvania became the vice-presidential candidate.

★  ★  ★  ★  ★  ★  ★  ★  ★  ★  ★  ★  ★  ★  ★  ★  ★  ★  ★  ★  ★  ★  ★  ★

## First Lady Sarah Polk

James K. Polk married 20-year-old Sarah Childress on New Year's Day, 1824. Eight years younger than her husband, she had first met him when she was 12. Sarah was the daughter of a wealthy farmer. She was very well educated for a young woman of her time.

*Sarah Childress Polk*

The couple had no children but were devoted to each other. Sarah played an important role in Polk's career, serving as his personal secretary and always seeking to build support for him. She had very firm views on what was proper and what was not. While the Polks were in the White House, dancing and alcoholic drinks were not allowed. Nor, on Sundays, was music, although Sarah herself very much enjoyed it.

Despite what may seem like a stern personality, Sarah Polk evidently had great charm. Senator Charles Sumner said, "Her sweetness of manner won me entirely." Justice Joseph Story of the Supreme Court wrote her a poem:

> For I have listened to thy voice, and watched the play-ful mind, Truth in its noblest sense thy choice, yet gentle, peaceful, kind.

Sarah Polk long outlived her husband. She died on August 14, 1891, at the age of 87.

---

The Democrats stressed the Texas and Oregon issues. They used the slogan "Fifty-four forty or Fight!" which referred to the degree of latitude that they thought the United States should claim as its border in Oregon.

The Whigs played on Polk's lack of a popular reputation. "Who is James K. Polk?" they asked. The Whigs nominated Henry Clay and New Jersey's Theodore Frelinghuysen. Clay had already made clear his opposition to annexing Texas. A third party, the Liberty party, chose James G. Birney of Michigan and

*Vice-President
George M. Dallas*

Thomas Morris of Ohio.  The Liberty party was against the spread of slavery.  Both Polk and Clay owned slaves, although only the Democrats made a point of saying that Congress should not interfere with slavery.

The election results were extremely close.  It took many days for the outcome to be clear.  James Polk had 50 percent of the popular vote and 170 electoral votes to Henry Clay's 48 percent and 105 electoral votes.  Although it got only 2 percent of the popular vote, the Liberty party actually elected Polk by taking votes away from Clay in New York, so Polk won the state.  Clay would have been elected president if he had carried it.

## Polk as President

Polk was only 49 years old, two years younger than Tyler, when he was inaugurated in the rain on March 4, 1845.  That made him the youngest president up to that time.  Polk worked very hard at fulfilling his responsibilities of being president.  He started very early in the day and worked late.  He wrote to his mother in December 1846: "My official term has nearly half expired.  My responsibilities and cares are very great, and I shall rejoice . . . when I can bid adieu to public life forever."

Early in his term, Polk had made clear what his goals were.  By then, the annexation of Texas had been accomplished.  He stated four objectives: "one, reduction of the tariff; another, the independent treasury; a third, the settlement of the Oregon boundary question; and lastly, the acquisition of California."

The Democrats were strong enough in Congress to carry out Polk's wishes on the tariff and the Independent Treasury.  They

★ ★ ★ ★ ★ ★ ★ ★ ★ ★ ★ ★ ★ ★ ★ ★ ★ ★ ★ ★ ★ ★ ★ ★

achieved both goals in 1846. Tariff rates were significantly lowered. The Independent Treasury Act restored the system for
holding the government's money—a system that Van Buren had
gotten passed in 1840 but that the Whigs had repealed in 1841.
This system remained the basis of the U.S. government's banking
system until 1913.

On the Oregon issue, President Polk modified his position.
The Oregon Territory was a huge region in the Pacific Northwest
between latitudes 54°40' and 42°. An 1818 agreement with
Britain had provided for joint occupation of the territory. But for
several years, American settlers had been moving into the region.
Some Americans, including Polk, began to demand that the
United States take over the entire territory. In connection with
both Texas and Oregon, journalists and congressmen used the
term *manifest destiny* to refer to what they thought was America's
"right . . . to spread over this whole continent."

Despite his earlier stand, Polk worked out a compromise
with Britain in 1846. The boundary between Canada and the
United States was set at latitude 49°. The states of Washington
and Oregon were later created out of the American portion.

## The Mexican War

Polk also achieved his goal of acquiring California, but only as a
result of a war with Mexico. California was then part of Mexico.
Americans had been settling in California for about 20 years. In
1845, several clashes took place there between American and
Mexican forces. The war with Mexico, however, started over Texas.

The annexation of Texas by the United States had created
bad relations with Mexico. The border between Mexico and
Texas was disputed. In late 1845, Polk sent a diplomatic mis-
sion to Mexico to attempt to resolve the dispute and to buy
California and what is now New Mexico. But Mexico refused to

★ ★ ★ ★ ★ ★ ★ ★ ★ ★ ★ ★ ★ ★ ★ ★ ★ ★ ★ ★ ★ ★ ★

*Mexican and U.S. troops fought at the Battle of San Gabriel in California.*

negotiate. Then, in January, Polk ordered troops in Texas, under General Zachary Taylor, to move south across the Nueces River into the disputed land. Mexican forces came north across the Rio Grande and fired on the American soldiers.

Polk then asked Congress for a declaration of war against Mexico. The president said that "Mexico has passed the boundary of the United States, has invaded our territory and shed American blood upon the American soil." Congress overwhelmingly passed the declaration by May 13, 1846.

The war was a triumph for America. In Mexico, Generals Taylor and Winfield Scott won several major battles. Scott occupied the Mexican capital of Mexico City in September 1846. General Stephen Kearney captured Santa Fe and then moved into California. By January 1847, all of California was in American hands.

★  ★  ★  ★  ★  ★  ★  ★  ★  ★  ★  ★  ★  ★  ★  ★  ★  ★  ★  ★  ★  ★  ★  ★  ★  ★

The Treaty of Guadalupe Hidalgo ended the war in February 1848. Mexico agreed to the Rio Grande as the southern border of Texas and ceded a vast region to the United States. From it, the states of California and New Mexico and parts of Arizona, Colorado, Nevada, and Utah would be created. In return, the United States paid Mexico more than $3 million and agreed to pay claims made by Americans against Mexico.

The war with Mexico, however, had some ominous consequences for the United States. It worsened the division over slavery between the North and the South. Northern congressmen tried to pass what became known as the Wilmot Proviso, after Congressman David Wilmot of Pennsylvania. It said that slavery shall never "exist in any part" of the lands won from Mexico. The Wilmot Proviso passed in the House of Representatives several times but was always defeated in the Senate.

## Polk Retires

Polk was glad to leave the presidency. He wrote in his diary on the day his term ended: "I feel exceedingly relieved that I am now free from all public cares. I am sure I shall be a happier man in my retirement than I have been during the four years I have filled the highest office in the gift of my countrymen."

Extremely tired, he nevertheless went on a month-long tour of the South before returning to his home near Nashville. In New Orleans he fell ill, possibly of cholera. Back home, he continued to weaken. On June 15, 1849, Polk died. He was not yet 54 years old.

★ ★ ★ ★ ★ ★ ★ ★ ★ ★ ★ ★ ★ ★ ★ ★ ★ ★ ★ ★ ★ ★ ★ ★ ★ ★

*The capture of Mexico City by General Winfield Scott in 1846 was one sign of the growing power of the United States.*

# 7

★  ★  ★

# The Presidency in an
# Era of Growth

Presidents have different impacts on their times.  Some dominate and shape their eras.  Others are driven by what is going on around them.  In the years 1829 to 1849, the United States was rapidly changing and growing:  Its population, its production of crops and manufactured goods, its roads, canals, and railroads, and its land area all increased significantly.  The office of the president also changed during this period.

Andrew Jackson was a very strong president.  Even though he frequently faced fierce opposition in Congress and elsewhere, he often got his way.  He insisted that South Carolina obey federal law, and it did.  He was determined to crush the Second Bank of the United States, and he did.

Jackson's significance, however, was greater than that.  He came into office at a time when the political process, like the nation as a whole, was changing.  In the 1828 election, more

*A log cabin—to show that he was a simple man—was the symbol of Harrison's presidential campaign.*

people could vote than ever before. No longer did a person have to own a certain amount of property to be allowed to vote. Jackson changed the office of the presidency. He saw himself as a spokesman for all Americans. As the people's voice, he was willing to use the powers of the presidency, such as the veto, in a way no president had before. He warned Americans about the corruption that great wealth can bring. He made it clear that he believed that there was nothing mysterious about government service—any reasonable person could do it.

Not all of the presidents who followed Jackson agreed with his conception of the office. But Jackson set the model for all the great presidents to come. His supporter and successor, Martin Van Buren, agreed with Jackson on most issues and was a very experienced politician. Van Buren, however, did not have Jackson's popular appeal. In addition, he inherited serious economic problems that Jackson's policies, in part, had helped bring about.

In 1840, the Whig party tried to make their candidate, William Henry Harrison, into another Andrew Jackson. In so doing, they changed forever how American presidential elections are run.

The 1840 election was the first great "spectacle election." The Whig campaign managers deliberately set out to create a certain image for Harrison. They wanted voters to think he was a simple man of the people, an honest farmer who just happened to be a military hero. In short, they wanted people to think that Harrison was another Jackson. So they held parades and made up songs and invented stories. And they elected their man.

Unfortunately, Harrison died a month after taking office. His successor, John Tyler, was not a Whig and would not go along with the Whig program. His major policy achievement, the annexation of Texas, was something that most Whigs opposed. Tyler did set the important precedent that when a president dies, the vice-president becomes the new president.

In 1844, the Democrats returned to power when James K. Polk was elected president. Polk did not have Jackson's personality, but—unlike Jackson, Van Buren, and Tyler—he had a friendly Congress to deal with. That, combined with his intelligence and hard work, enabled Polk to realize all of his major goals.

Most significant for the future of the United States was the expansion of territory that took place during Polk's administration. The dispute with Britain over Oregon was peacefully settled. The problems with Mexico over California and Texas were not peacefully settled. But the Mexican War resulted in a huge increase in the size of the country, adding two large states and parts of four others.

Yet, except for Jackson, it seems that all the presidents of these years were dwarfed by the changes taking place around them. Although the country was growing in many ways, it was also heading toward a civil war between the North and the South.

The basic cause of the Civil War was slavery. And, looking back, it is clear that slavery was closely connected with the issues that concerned the presidents from Jackson to Polk. The tariff, nullification, Texas, the Mexican War, even banking policy—all of these questions were either directly caused or made more complicated by the differences between North and South. The biggest difference, of course, was slavery. The presidents that followed Polk would try, in vain, to resolve the problem.

*The invention of the telegraph in 1832 contributed to the growth of the nation.*

# GLOSSARY

**annex**  To add to or make a part of what already exists.

**dark horse**  A successful candidate who previously was little known and not expected to win.

**Electoral College**  The group of people that formally elects the president by casting electoral votes.  Members of the Electoral College are elected by popular vote of the people in each state.

**export**  To sell goods in another country, or a good that is sold in another country.

**immigration**  The movement of people to one country from another country in order to live there.

**import**  To buy goods from another country, or a good that is bought from another country.

**internal improvements**  Roads, canals, and railroads.

**manifest destiny**  The idea that it was America's right to expand across North America.

**nominating conventions**  Meetings held by political parties at which delegates from all around the country choose the parties' candidates for president and vice-president.

**nullification**  The idea that a state can invalidate a federal law.

**secede**  To withdraw from the Union.

**specie**  Gold and silver used as money, as opposed to paper money.

**spoils system**  The practice whereby newly elected public officials discharge their opponents' supporters and appoint their own followers to government jobs.

**states' rights**  The belief that the powers of the states are the most important part of the American political system and that increases in the power of the federal government would threaten people's liberty.

**tariff**  A tax on goods imported into a country.

**third parties**  Political parties, in addition to the two main parties, that arise from time to time and play a significant role in elections.

**veto power**  The president's constitutional power to reject a proposed law passed by Congress.  A two-thirds majority in each house of Congress can override the president's veto and enact the bill into law.

# CHRONOLOGY

| | |
|---|---|
| **1767** | Andrew Jackson is born. |
| **1773** | William H. Harrison is born. |
| **1782** | Martin Van Buren is born. |
| **1790** | John Tyler is born. |
| **1795** | James K. Polk is born. |
| **1828** | Jackson is elected president. |
| **1830s–1840s** | Many Native Americans are moved west along the Trail of Tears. |
| **1830** | Congress passes the Indian Removal Act. |
| **1832** | The nullification crisis occurs. |
| | Jackson vetoes the renewal of the charter of the Second Bank of the United States. |
| | Jackson is re-elected. |
| **1836** | Van Buren is elected president. |
| **1837** | The Panic of 1837 hurts the American economy. |
| **1840** | Van Buren is defeated for re-election by Harrison. |
| **1841** | Harrison dies in office; Tyler becomes president. |
| **1844** | Polk is elected president. |
| **1845** | Texas is annexed to the United States. |
| | Jackson dies. |
| **1846** | The Mexican War begins. |
| **1848** | The Treaty of Guadalupe Hidalgo ends the Mexican War. |
| **1849** | Polk dies. |
| **1861** | Tyler supports secession of the South. |
| **1862** | Tyler dies. |
| | Van Buren dies. |

# TIMELINE

## •1770•

**1774** First Continental Congress

**1775** American Revolution begins

**1776** America declares independence from Great Britain

## •1780•

**1783** Treaty of Paris formally ends American Revolution

**1787** U.S. Constitution is written

1789 George Washington becomes president

## •1790•

**1791** Bill of Rights becomes part of Constitution

**1793** Eli Whitney invents cotton gin

1797 John Adams becomes president

## •1800•

Washington, D.C., becomes permanent U.S. capital

1801 Thomas Jefferson becomes president

**1803** Louisiana Purchase almost doubles size of the United States

**1808** Slave trade ends

1809 James Madison becomes president

## •1810•

**1812** War of 1812 begins

**1814** British burn Washington, D.C.
War of 1812 fighting ends

**1815** Treaty of Ghent officially ends War of 1812

1817 James Monroe becomes president

## •1820•

Missouri Compromise is passed

**1823** Monroe Doctrine is issued

1825 John Quincy Adams becomes president

**1828** Popular votes used for first time to help elect a president

1829 Andrew Jackson becomes president

## •1830•

Indian Removal Act is passed by Congress

**1832** Samuel Morse has idea for telegraph

**1835** Samuel Colt patents revolver

1837 Martin Van Buren becomes president

**1838** Native Americans are forced to move to Oklahoma traveling Trail of Tears

## •1840•

1841 William Harrison becomes president
John Tyler becomes president

1845 James Polk becomes president
Texas is annexed to United States

**1846** Mexican War begins
Boundary between Canada and United States is decided

**1848** Gold is discovered in California
First women's rights convention is held

1849 Zachary Taylor becomes president

## •1850•

Millard Fillmore becomes president
Compromise of 1850 is passed

1853 Franklin Pierce becomes president

1857 James Buchanan becomes president

## •1860•

Southern states begin to secede from Union

1861 Abraham Lincoln becomes president

**1863** Abraham Lincoln gives Gettysburg Address

1865 Andrew Johnson becomes president
Civil War ends
Freedmen's Bureau is created
13th Amendment abolishes slavery

**1868** Impeachment charges are brought against President Johnson

1869 Ulysses S. Grant becomes president

## •1870•

**1873** U.S. economy collapses; depression begins

**1876** Alexander Graham Bell invents telephone

1877 Rutherford Hayes becomes president

**1879** Thomas Edison invents lightbulb

## •1880•

1881 James Garfield becomes president
Chester Arthur becomes president

**1882** Chinese Exclusion Act restricts number of Chinese immigrants allowed into United States

1885 Grover Cleveland becomes president

1889 Benjamin Harrison becomes president

| 1890 | U.S. troops kill more than 200 Sioux and Cheyenne at Wounded Knee | 1930 | | 1970 | First Earth Day is celebrated |
|---|---|---|---|---|---|
| 1893 | Grover Cleveland becomes president again. Charles and J. Frank Duryea construct first car in the United States | 1933 | Franklin Roosevelt becomes president | 1973 | OPEC places oil embargo; fuel shortages result |
| | | | | 1974 | Nixon is first president to resign. Gerald Ford becomes president |
| 1897 | William McKinley becomes president | | | 1975 | War in Vietnam ends |
| 1898 | Spanish-American War occurs | | | 1976 | America celebrates its bicentennial |
| | | 1939 | World War II begins | 1977 | James Carter becomes president |
| 1900 | | 1940 | | 1978 | Camp David Accords are signed by leaders of Israel and Egypt |
| 1901 | Theodore Roosevelt becomes president | 1941 | Pearl Harbor is bombed; America enters World War II | 1979 | U.S. embassy in Iran is attacked and hostages are taken |
| 1903 | Orville and Wilbur Wright fly their plane at Kitty Hawk, North Carolina | | | 1980 | |
| | | | | 1981 | Ronald Reagan becomes president. American hostages are released. Reagan appoints first woman to Supreme Court, Sandra Day O'Connor |
| | | 1945 | Harry Truman becomes president. United States drops atomic bombs on Hiroshima and Nagasaki; World War II ends. United Nations is formed | 1986 | U.S. space shuttle Challenger explodes after lift-off |
| 1908 | Henry Ford produces Model T | | | | |
| 1909 | William Taft becomes president | | | 1989 | George Bush becomes president |
| 1910 | | 1950 | Korean War begins | 1990 | |
| | | | | 1991 | Persian Gulf War occurs |
| 1913 | Woodrow Wilson becomes president | 1953 | Dwight Eisenhower becomes president. Korean War ends | 1992 | U.S. troops are sent to Somalia to lead multinational relief force. Riots explode in Los Angeles |
| 1914 | Panama Canal opens | 1954 | Supreme Court orders desegregation of schools | 1993 | William Clinton becomes president. World Trade Center is bombed by terrorists |
| 1917 | America enters World War I | 1957 | Soviet Union launches Sputnik I | 1995 | Bomb destroys federal building in Oklahoma City |
| 1919 | World War I ends | 1958 | United States launches Explorer I. NASA is created | | |
| 1920 | 19th Amendment gives women right to vote | 1960 | | 2000 | |
| 1921 | Warren Harding becomes president | 1961 | John Kennedy becomes president | | |
| | | 1962 | Cuban Missile Crisis | | |
| 1923 | Calvin Coolidge becomes president | 1963 | Lyndon Johnson becomes president. March on Washington | | |
| | | 1964 | Civil Rights Act of 1964 is passed | | |
| | | 1965 | First U.S. troops sent to Vietnam War | | |
| 1927 | Charles Lindbergh makes first nonstop flight across Atlantic | 1968 | Martin Luther King, Jr. is assassinated | | |
| 1929 | Herbert Hoover becomes president. Stock market crashes; America enters economic depression | 1969 | Richard Nixon becomes president. Neil Armstrong is first person to walk on moon | | |

# PRESIDENTS OF THE UNITED STATES

| President | Birth | Party | Term | Death |
|---|---|---|---|---|
| George Washington | February 22, 1732; Westmoreland Cty., VA | None | April 30, 1789- March 4, 1797 | December 14, 1799; Mt. Vernon, VA |
| John Adams | October 30, 1735; Braintree (Quincy), MA | Federalist | March 4, 1797- March 4, 1801 | July 4, 1826; Quincy, MA |
| Thomas Jefferson | April 13, 1743; Albemarle Cty., VA | Democratic- Republican | March 4, 1801- March 4, 1809 | July 4, 1826; Charlottesville, VA |
| James Madison | March 16, 1751; Port Conway, VA | Democratic- Republican | March 4, 1809- March 4, 1817 | June 28, 1836; Orange County, VA |
| James Monroe | April 28, 1758; Westmoreland Cty., VA | Democratic- Republican | March 4, 1817- March 4, 1825 | July 4, 1831; New York, NY |
| John Quincy Adams | July 11, 1767; Braintree (Quincy), MA | Democratic- Republican | March 4, 1825- March 4, 1829 | February 23, 1848; Washington, D.C. |
| Andrew Jackson | March 15, 1767; Waxhaw, SC | Democratic | March 4, 1829- March 4, 1837 | June 8, 1845; Nashville, TN |
| Martin Van Buren | December 5, 1782; Kinderhook, NY | Democratic | March 4, 1837- March 4, 1841 | July 24, 1862; Kinderhook, NY |
| William Harrison | February 9, 1773; Berkeley, VA | Whig | March 4, 1841- April 4, 1841 | April 4, 1841; Washington, D.C. |
| John Tyler | March 29, 1790; Charles City Cty., VA | Whig | April 4, 1841- March 4, 1845 | January 18, 1862; Richmond, VA |
| James Polk | November 2, 1795; Mecklenburg Cty., NC | Democratic | March 4, 1845- March 4, 1849 | June 15, 1849; Nashville, TN |
| Zachary Taylor | November 24, 1784; Orange Cty., VA | Whig | March 4, 1849- July 9, 1850 | July 9, 1850; Washington, D.C. |
| Millard Fillmore | January 7, 1800; Locke Township, NY | Whig | July 9, 1850- March 4, 1853 | March 8, 1874; Buffalo, NY |
| Franklin Pierce | November 23, 1804; Hillsborough, NH | Democratic | March 4, 1853- March 4, 1857 | October 8, 1869; Concord, NH |
| James Buchanan | April 23, 1791; Cove Gap, PA | Democratic | March 4, 1857- March 4, 1861 | June 1, 1868; Lancaster, PA |
| Abraham Lincoln | February 12, 1809; Hardin Cty., KY | Republican | March 4, 1861- April 15, 1865 | April 15, 1865; Washington, D.C. |
| Andrew Johnson | December 29, 1808; Raleigh, NC | Republican | April 15, 1865- March 4, 1869 | July 31, 1875; Carter County, TN |
| Ulysses Grant | April 27, 1822; Point Pleasant, OH | Republican | March 4, 1869- March 4, 1877 | July 23, 1885; Mount McGregor, NY |
| Rutherford Hayes | October 4, 1822; Delaware, OH | Republican | March 4, 1877- March 4, 1881 | January 17, 1893; Fremont, OH |
| James Garfield | November 19, 1831; Orange, OH | Republican | March 4, 1881- September 19, 1881 | September 19, 1881; Elberon, NJ |
| Chester Arthur | October 5, 1830; North Fairfield, VT | Republican | September 20, 1881- March 4, 1885 | November 18, 1886; New York, NY |

| President | Birth | Party | Term | Death |
|---|---|---|---|---|
| Grover Cleveland | March 18, 1837; Caldwell, NJ | Democratic | March 4, 1885-March 4, 1889; March 4, 1893-March 4, 1897 | June 24, 1908; Princeton, NJ |
| Benjamin Harrison | August 20, 1833; North Bend, OH | Republican | March 4, 1889-March 4, 1893 | March 13, 1901; Indianapolis, IN |
| William McKinley | January 29, 1843; Niles, OH | Republican | March 4, 1897-September 14, 1901 | September 14, 1901; Buffalo, NY |
| Theodore Roosevelt | October 27, 1858; New York, NY | Republican | September 14, 1901-March 4, 1909 | January 6, 1919; Oyster Bay, NY |
| William Taft | September 15, 1857; Cincinnati, OH | Republican | March 4, 1909-March 4, 1913 | March 8, 1930; Washington, D.C. |
| Woodrow Wilson | December 28, 1856; Staunton, VA | Democratic | March 4, 1913-March 4, 1921 | February 3, 1924; Washington, D.C. |
| Warren Harding | November 2, 1865; Corsica, OH | Republican | March 4, 1921-August 2, 1923 | August 2, 1923; San Francisco, CA |
| Calvin Coolidge | July 4, 1872; Plymouth, VT | Republican | August 3, 1923-March 4, 1929 | January 5, 1933; Northampton, MA |
| Herbert Hoover | August 10, 1874; West Branch, IA | Republican | March 4, 1929-March 4, 1933 | October 20, 1964; New York, NY |
| Franklin Roosevelt | January 30, 1882; Hyde Park, NY | Democratic | March 4, 1933-April 12, 1945 | April 12, 1945; Warm Springs, GA |
| Harry Truman | May 8, 1884; Lamar, MO | Democratic | April 12, 1945-January 20, 1953 | December 26, 1972; Kansas City, MO |
| Dwight Eisenhower | October 14, 1890; Denison, TX | Republican | January 20, 1953-January 20, 1961 | March 28, 1969; Washington, D.C. |
| John Kennedy | May 29, 1917; Brookline, MA | Democratic | January 20, 1961-November 22, 1963 | November 22, 1963; Dallas, TX |
| Lyndon Johnson | August 27, 1908; Stonewall, TX | Democratic | November 22, 1963-January 20, 1969 | January 22, 1973; San Antonio, TX |
| Richard Nixon | January 9, 1913; Yorba Linda, CA | Republican | January 20, 1969-August 9, 1974 | April 22, 1994; New York, NY |
| Gerald Ford | July 14, 1913; Omaha, NB | Republican | August 9, 1974-January 20, 1977 | |
| James Carter | October 1, 1924; Plains, GA | Democratic | January 20, 1977-January 20, 1981 | |
| Ronald Reagan | February 6, 1911; Tampico, IL | Republican | January 20, 1981-January 20, 1989 | |
| George Bush | June 12, 1924; Milton, MA | Republican | January 20, 1989-January 20, 1993 | |
| William Clinton | August 19, 1946; Hope, AR | Democratic | January 20, 1993- | |